REALLY JAZZY POTS

REALLY JAZZY POTS

Glorious Gift Ideas

Mickey Baskett

Sterling Publishing Co., Inc.
New York

Prolific Impressions Production Staff:

Editor in Chief: Mickey Baskett
Copy Editor: Phyllis Mueller
Graphics: Dianne Miller, Karen Turpin
Styling: Lenos Key
Photography: Jerry Mucklow
Administration: Jim Baskett

Library of Congress Cataloging-in-Publication Data
Baskett, Mickey.
  Really jazzy pots : glorious gifts ideas / Mickey Baskett.
       p. cm.
  Includes index.
  ISBN 1-4027-2439-X
1. Pottery craft. 2. Decoration and ornament. 3. China painting--Technique.
4. Ceramic tableware. I. Title.
  TT920.B36 2005
  745.594--dc22

                                                              2005003995

10 9 8 7 6 5 4 3 2 1

Published by Sterling Publishing Co., Inc.
387 Park Avenue South, New York, N.Y. 10016

© 2005 by Prolific Impressions, Inc.
Produced by Prolific Impressions, Inc.
160 South Candler St., Decatur, GA 30030

Distributed in Canada by Sterling Publishing
c/o Canadian Manda Group, 165 Dufferin Street
Toronto, Ontario, Canada M6K 3H6

Distributed in Great Britain by Chrysalis Books Group PLC,
The Chrysalis Building, Bramley Road, London W10 6SP, England

Distributed in Australia by Capricorn Link (Australia) Pty. Ltd.
P.O. Box 704, Windsor, NSW 2756 Australia

Printed in China

For information about custom editions, special sales, premium and corporate purchases, please contact Sterling Special Sales Department at 800-805-5489 or specialsales@sterlingpub.com.

Sterling ISBN 1-4027-2439-X

CONTENTS

Versatile, Useful & Decorative

Clay pots and saucers - those classic, inexpensive, widely available containers - are versatile surfaces for decorating that, as you can see from the array of projects in this book, can be used in a variety of ways. Of course, they make wonderful decorative containers for plants, but planters are only the beginning.

You'll find projects for making clay pot characters that serve as containers for pet treats and supplies, as garden ornaments, and as seasonal tabletop decorations. See how to make containers for a variety of household items, caddies for tools and art and office supplies, a lamp, wind chimes, patio accessories, and candle holders. Find a wealth of ideas for using pots for storing and serving food, tips for baking in clay containers, and a recipe for a no-bake dessert cake that's served in a pot.

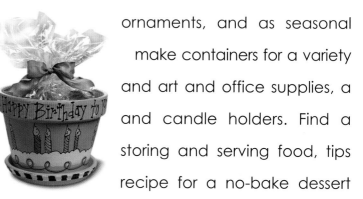

The projects showcase the work of six talented designers - Kathi Bailey, Patty Cox, Karen Embry, Kirsten Jones, Margaret Hanson-Maddox, and Barbara Mansfield - who have put their minds and hands to creating decorated pots for a variety of uses. There are more than three dozen projects - each with easy-to-follow, step-by-step instructions plus patterns, assembly diagrams, and photographs. Some projects use just one pot, some use a whole stack. Some are simple, and others are more ornate. The techniques used include painting, decoupage, stamping, stenciling, crackling, antiquing, and distressing. You'll find something interesting for everyone on your gift list, and some you will want to give yourself. Have fun!

Choosing a Pot

Clay pots have been used for centuries to cook and store food and beverages, to grow plants, and serve as containers for a variety of materials and objects. A clay container was also the original base vessel that is ceremoniously shattered of the piñata, the decorated to reveal its contents (treats, sweets, and gifts) during celebrations and religious observances in China, Italy, Spain, and Mexico.

The pots used to create the projects in this book are readily available at garden centers, hardware stores, home improvement centers, and department stores. A description and size (diameter) of the particular pot (or pots) is provided for each project.

Unglazed clay pots are manufactured in several countries, including Italy, the United States, Germany, Mexico, and Great Britain. They are made from a particular type of clay soil and fired in kilns to achieve their characteristic rusty brown color. New pots are best for decorating. Look for ones that are uniform in color and have a smooth, hard finish. Pass up pots with cracks or rough spots. If in doubt, thump the pot as you would a watermelon. It should make a ringing sound. (If it doesn't the pot may have a hairline crack.)

SUPPLIES
for Decorating Pots

PAINTS

Painting is an easy, quick way to transform a plain clay pot into a work of art or whimsy. Be sure to choose the right paint for the job.

Acrylic Craft Paints

Acrylic craft paints are richly pigmented, flat finish paints that come in plastic squeeze bottles and are especially made for decorative painting. They are available in a huge range of ready to use, pre-mixed colors, including rich metallics, glitters, and sparkles. Use them as base paints and for painting designs. Acrylic craft paints are not weather-resistant; if you are going to use your painted pot outdoors, be sure to apply a sealer after the paint is dry.

Mediums: Mediums are products specially designs to be used with the acrylic paints to alter their consistency, opaqueness, and performance. **Floating medium** is loaded onto the brush before the paint is loaded and it makes it more translucent so shadows and highlights can be "floated" onto the painted design. **Glazing medium** is mixed with the paint to create a glaze that is used to antique the finished design. **Blending medium** allows the paint to stay wet longer so that colors can be blended together.

Artist Tube Acrylics

Artist tube acrylic paints can also be used to paint designs on pots. Because they are thick, they must be mixed to a flowing consistency with water or a medium before painting. Artist tube acrylics also are not weather-resistant and so must be sealed if you plan to use your painted pot outdoors.

Outdoor Gloss Enamels

Indoor/outdoor gloss enamels are weather-resistant, durable acrylic paints. They dry to a glossy sheen and can be used outdoors without a protective finish. The number of pre-mixed colors is limited when compared with the color range of acrylic craft paints. No sealing is necessary.

Enamels for Glass & Ceramics

These enamels are acrylic paints that can be baked in a home oven to create a finish that is washable and top-rack dishwasher-safe. They provide opaque coverage and dry to a glossy sheen. Some brands of bakeable enamels can be air-cured; others must be baked to be permanent. Follow the manufacturer's instructions for use and curing.

FINISHES

To protect your decorated pot project, you'll need to coat it with some type of protective sealer. Be sure the one you choose is compatible with the paint you are using and that it will provide adequate protection in the place you will be using your pot.

Acrylic Aerosol Sealers

Aerosol finishes are clear-drying spray-on coatings that protect surfaces from moisture and dust. They are available in flat, satin, and gloss sheens. For best results, use several thin coats rather than one thick one. If you're using an aerosol finish on a pot you plan to use outdoors, be sure to choose one rated for outdoor use.

Brush-on Waterbase Finishes

Brush-on waterbase finishes (often called waterbase varnishes) are quick-drying, clear finishes you apply with a brush. They are available in a variety of sheens.

Brush-on Outdoor Sealers & Varnishes

Outdoor sealers (also called outdoor varnishes) are specifically designed for sealing and protecting surfaces that will be used outdoors. They are polyurethane based and clear-drying.

Decoupage Finish

Decoupage finish can be used to glue paper cutouts to pots and can be used to coat the pot for protection. Decoupage finish is not recommended as a sealer for a pot that is to be used outdoors or that will come into contact with moisture or liquids.

■ BRUSHES & APPLICATORS

Artist's Paint Brushes

Artist's paint brushes - flats, rounds, and liners - are used for painting designs and for lettering. Experienced painters recommend you use the best brushes you can afford and clean and care for them meticulously so they will last. Two good guidelines for choosing brushes are to use the size brush that fits the design and feels comfortable to you.

Stencil Brushes

When stenciling use brushes made especially for stenciling. They are tubular shaped with the bristles cut flat on end. The flat end allows you to "pounce" paint onto surface.

Foam Brushes

Foam brushes in the 1" size are handy for base painting and for applying crackle medium, decoupage finish, or glue. Foam rollers can also be used to paint pots.

Varnish Brushes

Varnish brushes are short-bristle brushes used for applying varnish. They come in a variety of widths.

Sponges

Sponges are useful for applying paint to create textures and designs. Compressed sponges, which you buy dry and flat, can be cut into shapes with scissors and hydrated to make sponge shapes for stamping.

Preparing Pots

SURFACE PREPARATION

1. Wash pots with vinegar and water to remove any dirt or oils. Scrub them with a brush if necessary. Let pots air dry completely.
2. If holes need to be drilled, use a carbide-tipped masonry drill bit. Make the holes *before painting or decorating*, in case the pot or saucer gets broken or develops a crack during drilling.
3. Paint the project according to the individual project instructions.
4. When paint is dry, apply the varnish of your choice to protect the painting.

TRANSFERRING PATTERNS

The patterns for the projects that require them are located on pages adjacent to the project. Follow this procedure to transfer a pattern to your pot:

1. Trace the pattern from the book onto **tracing paper**. Enlarge or reduce, if necessary on a photocopier so the design fits your intended pot.
2. Position the traced pattern on your project. Slip **transfer paper**, shiny side down, between the project and the traced pattern.
3. Re-trace the pattern lines *lightly* with a **stylus** to transfer the design.

SOME CAUTIONS

- **Planting in a Clay Pot.** *Do not* paint the insides of pots if you plan to plant live plants directly in the pot. That said, we recommend you *not* plant directly in the pot. For best results, and to preserve your painting, place another pot inside your painted pot to hold plants.

- **Waterproofing Pots.** If you plan to place any wet substance inside your decorated pot, we recommend you seal the inside of the pot with an outdoor varnish or a two-part resin coating. Clay is porous, and any liquid inside the pot can seep through and damage your decoration if the inside is not sealed.

- **Using with Food.** If you are using pots to present or store food, *do not* allow the food to come into contact with a painted surface. Use plastic liners, glass containers, or plastic bags to contain foods if the pot is painted on the inside. (It's okay for food to contact a clean, unpainted clay surface.)

Planters & Outdoor Pots

With a little paint and some clever techniques and patterns, you can decorate clay pots that are pretty enough to be used indoors or given as gifts.

Pictured at right: Weathered Welcome Tea Light Group. Instructions begin on page 14.

Pots:

4 standard pots, 3-1/2"

3 standard pots, 2-1/2"

Paints, Mediums & Finishes:

Acrylic craft paints:

Black

Pink

Moon Yellow

Aqua

Turquoise

Crackle medium (find this product in a craft shop where finishes are displayed)

Clear acrylic sealer

Tools & Other Supplies:

Sandpaper

Transfer paper, tracing paper, & stylus

Foam brushes for base painting and applying crackle medium

Artist brushes for painting lettering

WEATHERED WELCOME
tea light group

These small pots hold tea light candles and spell out the word "Welcome," which is painted over the rustic crackle finish. Use them to light a path or step in your garden.

By Patty Cox

INSTRUCTIONS

1. Base paint pots with Moon Yellow. Let dry.

2. Apply crackle medium according to manufacturer's instructions. Let dry.

3. Topcoat pots with Pink, Aqua, and Turquoise, using the photo as a guide for color placement. Allow paint to dry and form cracks.

4. Sand pots, allowing more of the base paint and some of the terra cotta to show. Wipe away dust.

5. Transfer letters to each pot.

6. Paint letters with Black. Let dry.

7. Spray with clear acrylic sealer. Let dry. ❏

Pattern for Weathered Welcome
Tea Light Group

WEL COME

CLAY POT FACTS

In the southeastern United States, fragments of clay pots have been found that date back to 2500 BC. Many of the pots found have patterns on them. The patterns help archaeologists determine when and by whom the pots were made. The pots found were tempered with steatite, then vegetable matter, then sand.

SUPPLIES

Pot & Saucer:

Tall clay pot, 6"

Clay saucer, 6"

Paints, Mediums & Finishes:

Acrylic craft paint - Orange

Antiquing medium - Brown

Brush-on high gloss finish

Tools & Other Supplies:

Anaglyptic wallpaper (wallpaper with a raised pattern but no color)

Scissors

100 grit sandpaper

Foam brush

Clear waterproof glue *or* silicone sealer

3 wooden ball knobs, 1-1/4" (for feet)

White craft glue

Cellulose sponge

TUSCAN TERRA COTTA
planter with base

By Kathi Bailey

INSTRUCTIONS

Adhere Wallpaper & Feet:

1. Cut out a raised design from the Anaglypta wallpaper to fit around rim. It can be pieced to fit if needed.

2. Adhere wallpaper to rim, following manufacturer's instructions. Use craft glue as needed to secure any loose ends. Let dry thoroughly.

Paint & Antique:

1. Paint pot and saucer with Orange.

2. Dampen sponge. Use it to apply antiquing medium over pot and saucer.

3. Stain ball knob feet with antiquing medium. Let dry.

Finish:

1. Glue feet to bottom of saucer with waterproof glue.

2. Brush on two coats high gloss finish to pot and saucer. Let dry. ❑

SUPPLIES

Pot:

Standard pot, 10-1/2"

Paints & Finishes:

Acrylic craft paints:

  Aqua

  Cobalt

  Green Light

  Magenta

  Medium Yellow

  Red Light

  White

Acrylic sealer

Tools & Other Supplies:

Transfer paper, tracing paper, & stylus

Foam brush for base painting

Artist brushes for painting design and lettering

CARIBBEAN SPIRIT
painted planter

By Patty Cox

INSTRUCTIONS

1. Base paint outside of pot with Red Light. Let dry.

2. Transfer patterns.

3. Paint sun rays on top rim with Medium Yellow.

4. Paint wavy line with Green Light. Add Aqua dots.

5. Paint lower border with Magenta.

6. Paint tiles with Aqua. Paint tile borders with Medium Yellow.

7. Paint the center diamond in each tile with Green Light. Paint the borders around the diamonds with Cobalt. Add strokes of White.

8. Paint lettering on the wavy line with Cobalt. Let dry.

9. Spray with clear acrylic sealer. ❑

Pattern appears on page 20.

Pattern for Caribbean Spirit Painted Planter

Instructions begin on page 19.

nature always wears the colors of the spirit—emerson

Pattern for Tropical Leaves Painted Planter

Instructions begin on page 23.

SUPPLIES

Pot:

Standard pot, 10"

Paints, Mediums & Finishes:

Indoor/outdoor gloss acrylic
  enamel - Oxblood

Acrylic craft paints:

  Black

  Green Dark

  Green Light

  Green Medium

  Red Light

Glazing medium

Acrylic sealer

Tools & Other Supplies:

Artist brushes, 1/2" flat and #12
  round

Glaze brush, 1-1/2" flat

Transfer paper, tracing paper, &
  stylus

Paper towel

Foam brush for base painting

TROPICAL LEAVES
painted planter

By Patty Cox

INSTRUCTIONS

Paint:

1. Base paint outside of pot with Oxblood using foam brush. Let dry.

2. Transfer leaf patterns to pot. Overlap some and place at different angles. Entire pot should be covered.

3. Paint large leaves with Green Light using the 1/2" flat brush.

4. Paint small leaves with a mix of Green Medium + Green Dark.

5. In the spaces between the leaves, dry brush Red Light comma strokes using the round brush. Let dry.

Glaze & Seal:

1. Mix 1 part black paint + 4 parts glazing medium. Dip a 1-1/2" flat brush in the mixture. Dab brush on a paper towel to remove excess. Dry brush streaks horizontally around pot. Let dry.

2. Spray with clear acrylic sealer. ❏

Pattern appears on page 21.

friends were flowers

SUPPLIES

Pot & Saucer:

Standard pot, 10" with matching
   saucer

Paints & Finishes:

Acrylic craft paints:

   Apricot

   Banana

   Black

   Pink

   Pool Blue

   Spring Green

Outdoor varnish

Tools & Other Supplies:

Artist brushes - #6, #12 flat

Tip-pen set (these are tips that fit
   onto the bottle opening, creating
   fine tips for lettering or detail
   work)

Transfer paper, tracing paper, &
   stylus

IF FRIENDS WERE FLOWERS
painted planter

By Kirsten Jones

INSTRUCTIONS

1. Base paint pot with Pink. Base paint rim and saucer with Black. Let dry.

2. Paint over black on rim with Spring Green. Paint over black on saucer with Pool Blue. Let black show through the brush strokes.

3. Transfer pattern to pot, repeating to fit.

4. Paint children, using the photo as a guide for color placement. Mix White and Apricot to create face color. Let dry.

5. Add details and words with Black, using the craft tip set on the paint bottle and following the craft tip manufacturer's instructions for use. Let dry.

6. Seal with outdoor varnish. Let dry. ❑

Pattern appears on pages 26-27.

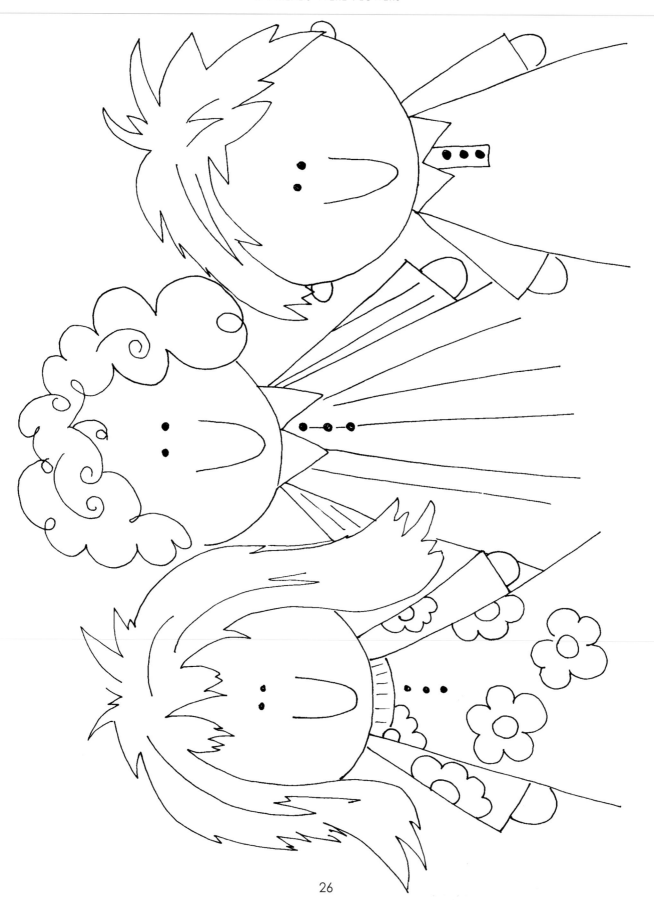

Pattern for If Friends Were Flowers
Painted Planter

If friends were flowers
I would Pick you...

FROG & BUTTERFLY
painted planter

By Karen Embry

INSTRUCTIONS

Base Paint:

Base paint both pots with Wicker White. Let dry.

Paint Frog:

1. Transfer the outlines of the frog. Basecoat the frog with the 1/2" flat using a mix of equal amounts Fresh Foliage + Yellow Light. Let dry.

2. Transfer the design details.

3. Float around the inside of the front legs and under the mouth with the 1/4" angled shader using Fresh Foliage. Float around the outsides of the front legs with Green Forest.

4. Paint the dots with the liner using a mix of equal amounts of Fresh Foliage + Green Forest.

5. Float over the eyelids with Green Forest. Float the top of the eyelids with Yellow Light. Float the bottom edges of the toes with Green Forest.

6. Paint the pupils, mouth, and eyelashes with Pure Black using the liner.

7. Paint the iris with Patina. Float with Azure Blue. Paint the highlights in the eyes and the white parts of the eyes with Wicker White.

8. Dry brush the nose and belly with Yellow Light using the hog bristle brush.

Paint Butterflies:

1. Paint one butterfly's wings with Baby Pink. Float the edges with Hot Pink. Paint the dots with Wicker White. Paint inside the dots with Hot Pink.

Continued on next page

29

Frog & Butterfly Painted Planter, continued from page 29

2. Paint the other butterfly's wings with Light Lavender. Float the edges with Violet Pansy. Paint the dots wit Wicker White. Paint inside the dots with Violet Pansy.

3. Paint the bodies on both butterflies with Cappuccino. Float with Burnt Sienna.

4. Paint the antennae with Pure Black.

Assemble:

1. Glue the butterfly pot to the frog pot. Let dry.

2. Spray with acrylic sealer. Let dry.

3. Glue bead trim to the top edge of the pot. Let dry. ❏

Patterns for Frog & Butterfly Painted Planter

Karen Embry

Patterns for Welcome Pineapple Stenciled Planter

Instructions begin on page 33.

SUPPLIES

Pot:

Standard clay pot, 10"

Paints, Mediums & Finishes:

Acrylic craft paints:

   Green Light

   Licorice

   Lipstick Red

   Yellow Ochre

Aerosol gloss finish

Tools & Other Supplies:

Foam brush for base painting

Stencil brush, 1/4"

Artist brush, #3 round

Stencil blank material

Craft knife or stencil cutting tool

Fine-tip black marker

Paper towel

How to Stencil: Dip the flat end of the stencil brush into a puddle of paint. Dab and rub brush in a circular motion on a paper towel to remove excess paint. Brush should look almost dry. Stencil in color by pouncing brush into stencil opening.

WELCOME PINEAPPLE
stenciled planter

By Kathi Bailey

INSTRUCTIONS

Base Paint:

Paint pot with Licorice. Let dry.

Stencil:

1. Trace patterns on stencil blank material with marker. Cut stencils, using a craft knife or stencil cutting tool.

2. Position stencils, using the photo as a guide. Stencil leaves and pineapple with Yellow Ochre, reversing the stencils as needed.

3. Paint flowers with the round brush using Lipstick Red. Make five teardrop shapes for petals.

4. Dot flower centers by dipping the end of a brush handle in Green Light. Dot paint onto surface. Let dry.

Finish:

Spray entire pot with gloss finish. ❏

Pattern appears on page 31.

POTTED HERBS
stenciled planters

These planter pots have been painted and then sanded to give them a warm distressed look. It is easy to add lettering to any pot using a stencil. To keep your pot in great condition, plant herbs in a separate pot that fits inside the painted pot.

By Kathi Bailey

Instructions begin on page 36.

SUPPLIES

Pots:

Standard clay pot, 8"

Standard clay pot, 6"

Paints, Mediums & Finishes:

Acrylic craft paints:

　Green Light

　Buttercup

Acrylic matte sealer spray

Tools & Other Supplies:

Foam brush for base painting

Stencil brush, 1/2"

Stencil blank material

Craft knife or stencil cutting tool

Fine-tip black marker

Paraffin wax stick

80 grit sandpaper

POTTED HERBS
stenciled planters

Pictured on page 34-35

INSTRUCTIONS

Base Paint:

1. Rub rim and parts of pot base with streaks of wax. This will make distressing easier. The paint will sand off easily from these wax coated areas.

2. Paint pots with two coats Green Light using foam brush. Let dry.

Distress:

Sand the pots to remove some of the paint, allowing the clay surfaces to show through. Wipe away dust with a damp cloth. Let dry.

Stencil:

See page 33 for "How to Stencil."

1. Trace patterns on stencil blank material with a marker. Cut stencils, using a craft knife or stencil cutting tool.

2. Stencil words on pots with Buttercup. Let dry.

Finish:

Spray pots with matte sealer. ❏

Patterns for Potted Herbs Stenciled Planters

SUPPLIES

Pot:

Standard clay pot, 8"

Paints & Finishes:

Acrylic craft paints:

    Asphaltum

    Burnt Umber

    Green Light

    Yellow Ochre

Acrylic matte sealer spray or
    outdoor varnish

Tools & Other Supplies:

Drywall Compound

Short stiff-bristle brush

Artist brush, 1-1/2" flat wash brush

Sandpaper

Paper towels

RUSTIC STUCCO
textured planter

Drywall compound and four earth-tone paint colors
add rustic texture to a clay pot.

By Kathi Bailey

INSTRUCTIONS

Prepare Pot:

Spray inside and outside of pot with matte sealer. Let dry.

Add Texture:

1. Apply a thick coat of drywall compound over the entire pot with a stiff-bristle brush, leaving brush marks. Let dry overnight.

2. Lightly sand. Brush off dust.

3. Apply a second coat of drywall compound with the bristle brush, making sure the brush marks show.

Paint:

1. Add water to Yellow Ochre to thin to a wash consistency. Apply over entire pot with large 1/2" flat brush.

2. Repeat the process with other colors listed, wiping off in small areas to show texture. Repeat colors as needed to darken. Let dry thoroughly.

Finish:

Spray entire pot with matte sealer or outdoor varnish. Let dry. ❏

SUPPLIES

Pot:

Standard clay pot, 6"

Paints & Finishes:

Acrylic craft paint:

   Coastal Blue

Acrylic matte sealer spray

Tools & Other Supplies:

Foam brush

Seashells (enough to cover the sides
   of the pot)

1 cup sand

Clear waterproof glue *or* silicone
   sealer

White craft glue

Glue brush

ENCRUSTED SEASHELLS
mosaic planter

Seashells and sand (reminiscent of a trip to the beach)
are glued to a pot. Use this pot indoors as the
glue would not withstand the weather.

By Kathi Bailey

INSTRUCTIONS

Paint:

Paint pot below the rim with Coastal Blue using foam brush. Let dry.

Add Shells & Sand:

1. Glue shells around sides of pot base with waterproof glue. TIP: Place the pot on its side and work one area at a time, rotating the pot so the shells do not slide off the pot. When pot is covered with shells as shown in photo, let dry overnight.

2. Use a glue brush to apply a thick layer of craft glue to open areas between the shells. While glue is still wet, sprinkle sand over all areas to cover the pot. Let dry. Repeat as needed, making sure all areas between the shells are covered with sand. Let dry completely.

Finish:

Spray entire pot with matte finish. Let dry. ❑

Clay Pot Characters

The clay characters in this section are colorful,
whimsical works of art created from an
assemblage of readily available pots and saucers.
To glue the pots together, it's necessary to use a
strong multi-purpose adhesive or silicone sealer.
Follow the adhesive manufacturer's instructions
for application and drying times, and work in
a well-ventilated area.

Pictured at right: Happy Cat Toys & Treats Pillar. Instructions begin on page 45.

SUPPLIES

Pots & Saucers:

3 azalea pots, 6"

1 clay saucer, 6"

1 clay saucer, 7"

Paints & Finishes:

Indoor/outdoor gloss acrylic enamels:

Black

Mustard

Oxblood

Terra Cotta

White

Clear acrylic sealer

Tools & Other Supplies:

Foam brush for base painting

Artist brush, #1 liner

1 child's tube sock (for front legs)

White felt

Strong multi-purpose glue

Sea sponge

Insulating foam sealant

Scissors

Transfer paper, tracing paper and stylus

Optional: Fabric glue, putty *or* grout, black fine-tip permanent marker

HAPPY CAT
toys & treats pillar

By Patty Cox

INSTRUCTIONS

Assemble:

Refer to diagrams on the following page.

1. Glue two 6" pots together at rims. See Fig. 1
2. Glue one 7" saucer to base.
3. Spray insulating foam sealant inside the small hole of the top pot. Fill the two glued pots a little over half full, using the spray nozzle stick as a gauge. The sealant will expand.
4. Paint tube sock with a wash of Mustard. Let dry.
5. Cut off toe of sock and reserve for ears. See Fig. 2. Tie a knot in the center of the tube sock.
6. Glue ends of tube sock on the top of the glued pots. Glue remaining 6" saucer on top. Allow glue to dry.
7. *Option:* Fill the gap between the top pot and the saucer with grout or putty. Let dry.

Paint:

1. Base paint all pots with Mustard using foam brush. Let dry.
2. Transfer pattern, using Fig. 3 as a guide.
3. Sponge mouth and cheek area with White using the sea sponge to pounce on the paint. Sponge stomach with White.
4. Sponge stripes with Terra Cotta and Oxblood.
5. Paint eyes and face details with Black, using a liner brush.*Option:* Add eyes and face details with a fine-tip marker.
6. Dot eye highlights with White paint.

Finish:

1. Cut reserved toe end of sock in half. Glue the wrong side of each piece to the white felt. Let dry.

Continued on next page

Happy Cat, continued from page 45.

2. Trim felt evenly around sock pieces.
3. Fold each ear in half and crease. Glue ears to head as shown. Let dry.
4. Spray all pieces with clear acrylic sealer. Let dry.
5. Place head pot on glued-together pots. ❏

Pattern for Happy Cat Face

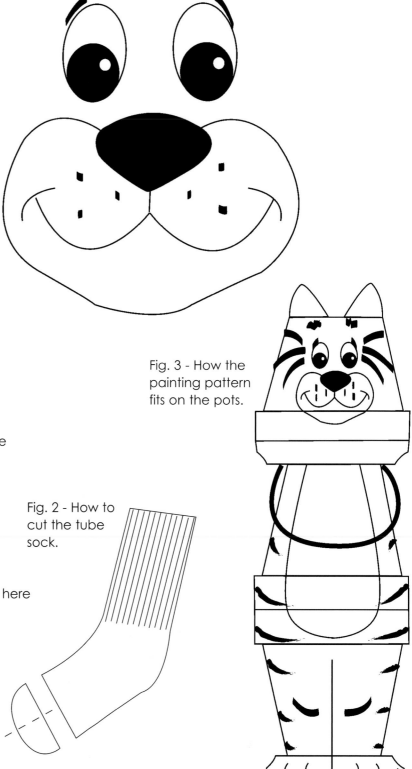

Fig. 3 - How the painting pattern fits on the pots.

Fig. 1 - Assembly diagram.

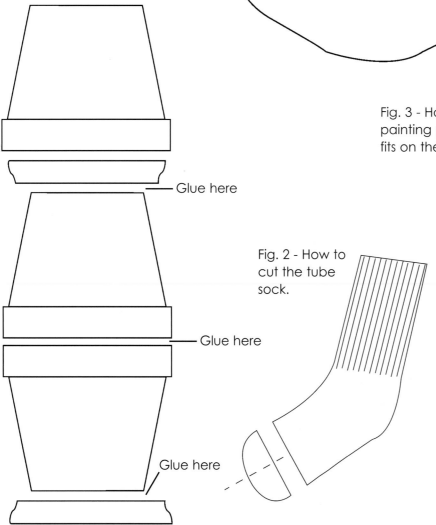

Glue here

Glue here

Fig. 2 - How to cut the tube sock.

Glue here

Patterns for Frisky Fido Toys & Treats Pillar

Instructions begin on page 48.

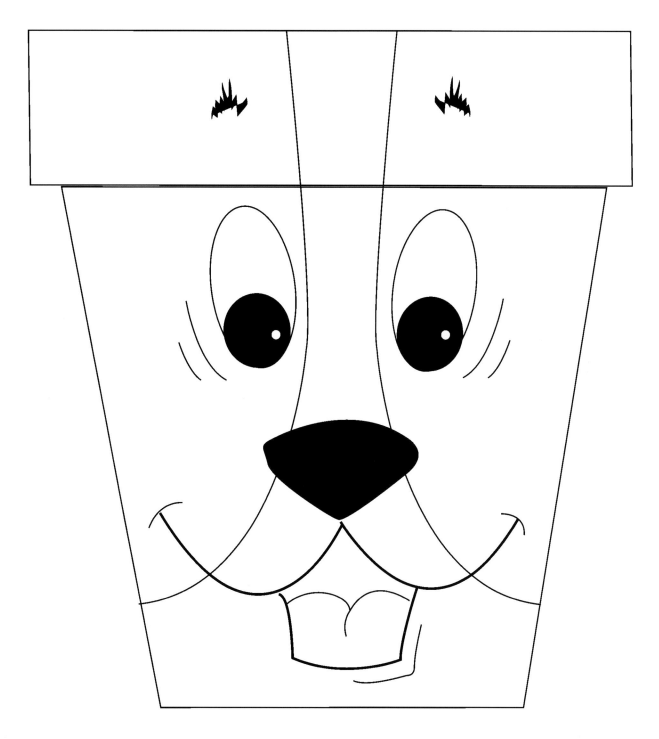

SUPPLIES

Pots & Saucers:
2 standard clay pots, 6"
1 azalea pot, 6"
2 clay saucers, 6"
Wooden flower pot, 1-3/4"

Paints & Finishes:
Acrylic craft paints:
Black   Green   Red
Terra Cotta   White
Clear acrylic sealer

Tools & Other Supplies:
Foam brush for base painting
Artist brushes, #1 liner, #4 round
Insulating foam sealant
Strong multi-purpose adhesive
1 white child's tube sock (for front
   legs)
2 black anklet socks (for ears)
Transfer paper, tracing paper and
   stylus
Optional: Black fine-tip permanent
   marker

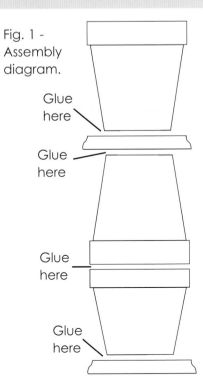

Fig. 1 -
Assembly
diagram.

Glue
here

Glue
here

Glue
here

Glue
here

FRISKY FIDO
toys & treats pillar

Use this pillar of pots to hold dog treats and toys. It will be your dog's favorite friend.

By Patty Cox

Fig. 2 - Diagram showing paint and decoration placement.

INSTRUCTIONS

Assemble:

1. Glue 6" standard pot and 6" azalea pot together at rims. Glue one 7" saucer base to azalea pot.

2. Spray insulating foam sealant inside the small hole of top pot. Fill the two glued pots a little over half full, using the spray nozzle stick as a gauge. The sealant will expand.

3. Paint the tube sock with a wash of Terra Cotta paint. Let dry.

4. Tie a knot at the center of the tube sock. Glue the tube sock ends on the top of the glued pots.

5. Glue the 6" saucer upside down over the top of the pots.

6. Glue the 6" standard pot on top of saucer, right side up. Allow glue to dry.

Paint:

1. Paint dog's body with Terra Cotta and White, using the photo and Fig. 2 for guides for color placement. Let dry.

2. Transfer face pattern from page 47.

3. Paint tongue with Red. Paint eyes with White. Paint nose with Black.

4. Paint collar (the top saucer) with Green.

5. Paint eyes and face and leg details with Black, using a liner brush. See the photo and Fig. 2 for leg details. *Option:* Add eyes and face details with a fine tip marker.

6. Dot eye highlights with White acrylic paint.

Finish:

1. Cut the cuffs off black socks. Glue socks on sides of top pot for ears as shown in photo.

2. Paint 1-3/4" wooden pot with Red. Let dry.

3. Write "TREATS" on pot using liner brush or fine-tip marker.

4. Spray with clear acrylic sealer. Let dry.

5. Place small pot in dog's front legs. ❑

SUPPLIES

Pots & Saucer:

3 standard pots, 2-1/2"

1 clay saucer, 3"

Paints & Finishes:

Acrylic craft paints:

    Cappuccino

    Dusty Peach

    Rose Pink

    Terra Cotta

    White

Clear acrylic sealer spray

Tools & Other Supplies:

Foam brush for base painting

Artist brushes, #4 flat, #4 round, #1 liner

12" peach grosgrain ribbon, 5/8" wide (for arms)

Strong multi-purpose adhesive

Black fine-tip permanent marker

Electronic music box

Pink tulle, 46" x 6"

Heavy duty pink thread

Plastic foam ball, 2-1/4"

Small pink-edged silk flowers

Insulating foam sealant

Powder blush makeup and cotton swab

Transfer paper, tracing paper, and stylus

LITTLE BALLERINA
music box

This ballerina wears a pink tulle tutu and silk flowers on her head. An electronic music box that plays "My Favorite Things" is glued under the saucer base.

By Patty Cox

INSTRUCTIONS

Assemble:

1. Glue the two 2-1/2" pots together at rims.

2. Glue one 3" saucer to base.

3. Spray insulating foam sealant inside the small hole of pot. Fill the two glued pots a little over half full, using the spray nozzle stick as a gauge. The sealant will expand.

4. Tie a knot in the center of the grosgrain ribbon. Glue ends of ribbon on the top of the glued pots.

5. Glue remaining 2-1/2" pot (the head) on top. Allow glue to dry.

Paint:

1. Base paint all pots with Dusty Peach. Let dry.

2. Transfer pattern to pots.

3. Float Cappuccino shading on skin to contour, using the pattern marks as a guide. Use the #4 flat brush.

4. Paint leotard and shoes with Rose Pink.

5. Paint hair with Terra Cotta.

6. Draw eyes and face detail with fine-tip marker.

7. Dot eye highlights with White acrylic paint.

Continued on next page

Little Ballerina, continued from page 51

8. Rub cheeks with powdered blush.

9. Spray with clear acrylic sealer. Let dry.

Make TuTu:

1. Fold tulle lengthwise in half, then fold lengthwise in half again. Press folds with a warm iron.

2. Open one fold. Gather tulle with threads along center crease.

3. Place tutu on ballerina. Pull gathers tightly around ballerina. Tie off gathering threads.

Finish:

1. Glue 2-1/4" foam ball in top of head pot.

2. Pull the flowers off the stems. Glue and stick flowers in foam ball, covering the top of the head. *Optional:* Glue a flower at knot in ballerina's hands.

3. Glue music box under saucer base as shown in photo. ❏

Music box is glued under saucer.

Pattern and Assembly Diagram for Little Ballerina Music Box

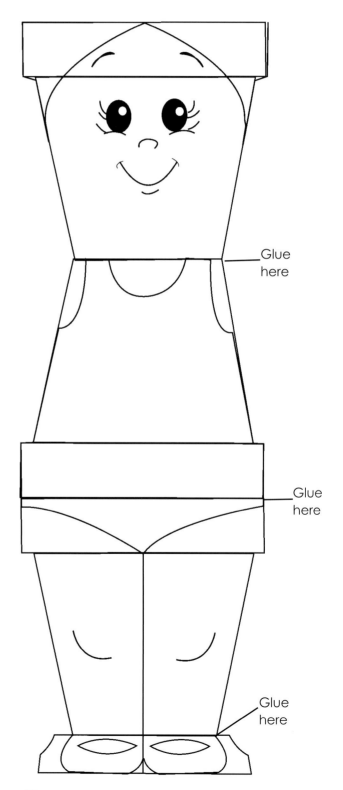

Glue here

Glue here

Glue here

Pattern for Pumpkin Surprise Treat Container

Instructions begin on page 55.

SUPPLIES

Pot & Saucers:

Clay pot, 6-1/2"

2 clay saucers, 7-1/2"

Paints, Mediums & Finishes:

Acrylic craft paints:

    Azure Blue

    Metallic Gold

    Patina

    Pumpkin

    Pure Black

    Pure Orange

    Tangerine

    Wicker White

    Yellow Light

Glazing medium

Floating medium

Acrylic matte sealer spray

Tools & Other Supplies:

Artist brushes - 1/4" and 1/2" angled shaders, 10/0 liner, #5 round

Foam brush for base painting

Transfer paper, tracing paper, and stylus

Round wooden knob with one flat side, 2" diameter

24" beaded orange trim

Thick white glue

Cement screw

Drill with tile drill bit

PUMPKIN SURPRISE
treat container

Use this container to hold Trick-or-Treat goodies or as part of a table centerpiece.

By Karen Embry

INSTRUCTIONS

Paint:

1. Base paint the pot and saucers with Tangerine using the foam brush. Let dry.

2. Apply a coat of glazing medium to the pot and saucers. Brush on some Pumpkin, trying not to cover the base paint entirely. While it is still wet, brush on Yellow Light in some areas and Pure Orange in others. Slightly blend the colors where they meet, but try not to over blend. Let dry.

3. Transfer the face pattern from page 53.

4. Basecoat the nose, mouth, and pupils with Pure Black. Float the top of the nose with a mix of equal amounts of Pure Black + Wicker White using an angled shader. *See page 29 for "How to Float."*

5. Basecoat the irises with Patina. Float them with Azure Blue. Paint the whites of the eyes with Wicker White.

6. Outline the eyes and paint the eyelashes with Pure Black. Paint the highlights on the eyes, nose, and mouth with Wicker White.

7. Paint the wooden knob with Metallic Gold. Let dry.

Finish:

1. Drill a small hole in the bottom center of one saucer. Use glue and the cement screw to attach the knob to saucer. Glue the painted pot to the bottom of the other saucer. Use the photo as a guide.

2. Spray the pot and saucers with two coats of matte acrylic sealer. Let dry.

3. Glue the beaded trim around the top edge of the pot as shown. ❏

SUPPLIES

Pots:

2 standard clay pots, 4"

1 clay pot with narrow rim, 2-1/2"

1 standard clay pot, 2"

2 clay pot feet

Paints & Finishes:

Acrylic craft paints:

   Azure Blue

   Coastal Blue

   Licorice

   Warm White

   Yellow Ochre

Acrylic matte sealer spray

Tools & Other Supplies:

Foam brush for base painting

Clear waterproof glue

Drill and 1/4" glass and tile drill bit with arrowhead design

Artist brushes - #3 round, liner

2 stones (similar size and shape)

2 yds. copper wire

Wire cutters and pliers

Dowel

GOONY BIRD
garden character

By Kathi Bailey

INSTRUCTIONS

Drill:

1. Mark two spaces, one on each side of one 4" pot near the bottom, for the wings. Drill holes.

2. Mark and drill two holes for the tail near the bottom of the other 4" pot.

Glue:

1. Glue the two 4" pots together at the rims to make the body.

2. Glue the 2" pot into the rim of the 2-1/2" pot for the head.

3. Glue head on top of body.

4. Glue two feet (the pot feet) on the front of body at bottom.

Paint:

1. Paint body with Coastal Blue.

2. Paint 2" pot below the rim with Yellow Ochre. (This is the beak.)

3. Paint the rim of the 2-1/2" pot with Warm White.

4. Paint top of head and half the rim of the 2-1/2" pot with Azure Blue.

5. Paint breast of bird with Warm White, using the photo as a guide for color placement. Let dry. Transfer pattern for breast design from page 59.

6. Add scroll lines, using a liner brush with Licorice, on the breast. Paint a "V" on the beak.

7. Paint feet with Yellow Ochre.

Add Wings, Crest & Tail:

See the following pages for patterns.

1. Cut three 10" lengths of copper wire. Use the dowel to bend each piece of wire into three loops for the wings and tail, following the pattern shapes provided.

Continued on next page

continued from page 57

2. Use remaining wire to make a three-loop crest, following the pattern shape provided. Bend 1/4" with pliers at end.

3. Insert ends of wires for wings and tails in holes and glue to secure. Glue bent ends of crest into rim of head. Let dry.

Add Eyes:

1. Paint large ovals with Licorice on stones to make the eyes.

2. Glue stones over crest wire, using the photo as a guide for placement.

Finish:

Spray with matte finish. Let dry. ❏

Patterns for Goony Bird Garden Ornament

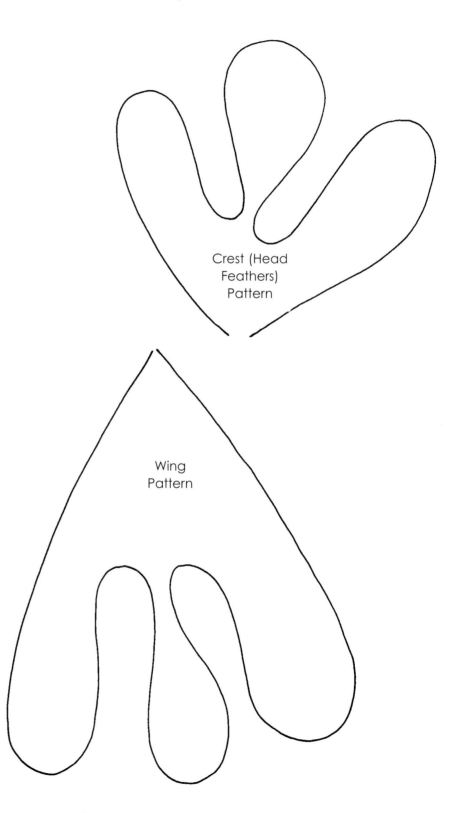

Crest (Head Feathers) Pattern

Wing Pattern

Breast Design
pattern

Tail Pattern

SUPPLIES

Pots:

5 terra cotta flower pots, 2-3/4"

Paints:

Acrylic craft paints:

    Burnt Umber

    White

    Flesh Tone

    Holly Green

    Light Cinnamon

    Mauve

    Payne's Grey

    Red

Acrylic gloss sealer spray

Tools & Other Supplies:

Artist brushes - #4 fabric scrubber, #12 flat shader, #4 round, 10/0 liner

Foam brush for base painting

Scissors

White art foam sheet, 3" x 4"

Wooden candle cup, 1"

Wooden gingerbread boy, 1"

Glue gun and glue sticks

Transfer paper, tracing paper, and stylus

White pom-pom, 2"

HOLIDAY SANTA
table decoration character

By Margaret Hanson-Maddox

INSTRUCTIONS

Paint Pots:

1. Using 1" foam brush, paint four pots with Red, leaving the rims unpainted.
2. Using a #12 flat shader, paint the remaining pot with Flesh Tone.
3. On two of the red pots, use the fabric scrubber to tap White paint on the rims.
4. On the remaining red pot, paint the rim with Payne's Grey.
5. Transfer face pattern from page 63 to Flesh Tone pot, using the photo as a guide for placement.
6. Using the fabric scrubber brush, tap White paint on the Flesh Tone pot for beard, moustache, and hair, leaving a 1" area for the neck.
7. Using a liner brush, add White eyebrows.
8. Using the fabric scrubber brush, apply Mauve to the cheek area.
9. Using liner brush, outline moustache with Payne's Grey.
10. Using a stylus, dot eyes with Payne's Grey.
11. Using a round brush, paint inner mouth with Red and lower lip with Mauve.
12. On one red pot with white rim, tap a White 1"-wide vertical band for center front fur.

Paint Arms:

1. Transfer pattern for arms to art foam sheet. Cut out.
2. Using a #12 flat shader, paint gloves with Holly Green and arms with Santa Red.
3. Using the fabric scrubber, tap white fur between the Red and Holly Green areas.

Paint Candle Cup & Gingerbread Man:

1. Using the #12 flat shader, paint candle cup with Red.
2. Using the #12 flat shader, paint gingerbread man with Light Cinnamon.
3. Dip one side of the flat shader in Light Cinnamon. Dip the opposite side in White. Highlight the right side of head, hand, and leg.

Continued on page 63

Santa on the Tree
ornament

By Margaret Hanson-Maddox

SUPPLIES

Pots:

5 terra cotta flower pots, 1"

Paints:

Acrylic craft paints:

  Burnt Umber

  White

  Flesh Tone

  Holly Green

  Light Cinnamon

  Mauve

  Payne's Grey

  Red

Acrylic gloss sealer spray

Other Tools & Supplies:

Artist brushes - #2 fabric scrubber, #8 flat shader, #2 round, 10/0 liner

Transfer paper, tracing paper, stylus

Scissors

White art foam sheet, 1" x 2"

Glue gun and glue sticks

White pom-pom, 1"

8" black rattail satin cording

INSTRUCTIONS

Paint:

1. Using #8 flat shader, paint four pots with Red, leaving the rims unpainted.
2. Using the same brush, paint the remaining pot with Flesh Tone.
3. On two of the red pots, use the fabric scrubber to tap White paint on the rims.
4. On the remaining red pot, paint the rim with Payne's Grey.
5. Transfer the pattern for the face to the Flesh Tone pot, referring to the photo for placement.
6. Using the fabric scrubber brush, tap White paint on the Flesh Tone pot for the beard, moustache, and hair, leaving a 3/8" area for neck.
7. Using a liner brush, add White eyebrows.
8. Using the fabric scrubber brush, apply Mauve to the cheek area.
9. Using the liner brush, outline the moustache with Payne's Grey. Using a stylus, dot eyes with Payne's Grey.
10. Using the round brush, paint the inner mouth with Red and the lower lip with Mauve.
11. On one red pot with a white rim, tap a White 3/8"-wide vertical band for center front fur.

Make & Paint Arms:

1. Transfer pattern for arms to art foam sheet. Cut out.
2. Using a #8 flat shader brush, paint gloves with Holly Green. Paint arms with Red.

Patterns for Santa on the Tree Ornament

Santa on the Tree, continued

3. Using the fabric scrubber, tap white fur between Red and Holly Green areas.

Assemble:

1. Referring to the photo, glue pots together to form hat, head, and body. Let dry.
2. Spray piece with sealer
3. Glue arms to each side of body.
4. Glue each end of rattail cording to top of hat.
5. Glue pom-pom to top over cording. ❑

Arm

Patterns for Holiday Santa Table Decoration

Holiday Santa, continued from page 61

4. Dip one side of the #12 flat shader in Burnt Umber. Dip the opposite side in Light Cinnamon. Shade the left side of the head, hand, and leg.
5. Using a liner brush, add White eyebrows and squiggly lines on arms and legs.
6. Using a stylus, add Payne's Grey dip-dot eyes.
7. Using the handle end of the liner brush, add three White buttons.

Assemble:

1. Using the photo as a guide, glue pots together to form hat, head, and body. Let dry.
2. Spray piece with sealer.
3. Glue arms to each side of body.
4. Glue the candle cup between the hands.
5. Glue gingerbread man to front of candle cup.
6. Glue pom-pom to top of Santa. ❑

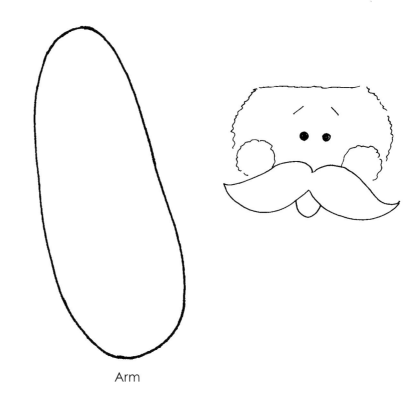

Arm

Not Just Planters

Clay pots can do so much more than hold plants. The 15 projects in this section illustrate the versatility of pots as gift containers, caddies for art supplies, office supplies, and kitchen tools, for holding candles, umbrellas, and patio torches, or assembled to make a wind chime.

Pictured at right: Happy Birthday Gift Pot. Instructions begin on page 66.

SUPPLIES

Pot & Saucer:

Medium clay pot

Medium clay saucer

Paints & Finishes:

Acrylic craft paints:

 Apricot

 Banana

 Black

 Fuchsia

 Petunia Purple

 Pool Blue

 Spring Green

 White

Outdoor varnish

Tools & Other Supplies:

Foam brush for base painting

Artist brushes - #6 and #12 flats

Tip-pen set (these are tips that fit onto the bottle opening, creating fine tips for lettering or detail work)

Transfer paper, tracing paper, and stylus

HAPPY BIRTHDAY
gift pot

A pot makes a great gift container - and it is also a gift. Wrap the present in clear cellophane, tie with a bow, and place in pot. The pot can be used later as a planter and will remind the recipient of your friendship.

By Kirsten Jones

INSTRUCTIONS

1. Basecoat pot with White. Let dry.

2. Transfer cake pattern repeating the design around the pot.

3. Paint bottom (cake) with Banana, frosting with White, and top (background) with Pool Blue.

4. Paint rim of pot with Fuchsia.

5. Paint saucer with Pool Blue. Let dry.

6. Paint candles with a variety of colors, using the photo as a guide.

7. Add swirl with Apricot. Let dry.

8. Add details and lettering with Black, using the craft tip set. Let dry.

9. Seal both pieces with varnish. Let dry. Place pot in saucer. ❏

Pattern for Happy
Birthday Gift Pot

Happy Birthday to you...

SUPPLIES

Pots & Saucer:
2 standard clay pots, 6"
1 clay saucer, 6"

Paints, Mediums & Finishes:
Acrylic craft paints:
   Black
   Buckskin Brown
   Burnt Umber
Glazing medium
Acrylic matte sealer spray

Tools & Other Supplies:
Foam brush for base painting
Stencil brush
Chamois faux finish tool or sponge
Cellulose sponge
Gold leaf sheets
Gold leaf adhesive
Glue brush
Stencil blank material
Craft knife
Black fine-tip marker
Clear waterproof glue *or* silicone
Drill and 1/4" glass and tile drill bit
   with arrowhead design
Lamp kit
All-thread lamp pipe kit for 12" lamp
Lampshade

Patterns for Leaves

GOLDEN LEAVES
lamp

By Kathi Bailey

INSTRUCTIONS

Prepare Pots & Saucer:
1. Turn over saucer. Center the bottom of one pot on the saucer and mark. Mark the place for the wire hole on the side of the saucer.
2. Drill center hole and wire hole in saucer.
3. Glue two pot rims together, one atop the other.
4. Glue bottom of one pot to overturned saucer to make the base, lining up the holes.

Base Paint:
1. Paint pots with Buckskin Brown.
2. Paint saucer with Black.

Glazing:
1. Mix 3 parts glazing medium and 1 part Burnt Umber.
2. Brush mixture on pots. Dab with Chamois faux finishing tool or sponge to remove some of the glaze and create a textured look.

Stencil & Apply Gold Leaf:
1. Trace patterns on stencil blank with marker. Cut out patterns, using a craft knife.
2. Position stencils on pots, scattering them over the lamp base, and apply gold leaf adhesive through the stencil openings using a stencil brush to pounce in adhesive. Apply glue over entire saucer base. Let dry according to the manufacturer's instructions.
3. Apply gold leaf over adhesive on pots and saucer base.
4. Dampen a cellulose sponge. Wipe lamp and base with glazing mixture. Let dry.

Finish:
1. Spray entire pot with matte finish.
2. Use the lamp kit and lamp pipe kit to wire the lamp, following the kit manufacturers' instructions.
3. Install shade. ❑

Pot:

1 gallon clay strawberry pot

Paints, Mediums & Finishes:

Decoupage finish

Acrylic craft paint:

   Aqua

Acrylic sealer

Tools & Other Supplies:

Old map

Old postcards and/or photographs, copied and reduced on a color photocopier

Rubber stamps:

   Postmark

   Compass

Black permanent ink pad

Black construction paper

Foam brush for base painting

ARTIST'S ASSISTANT
art supplies caddy

Cover a strawberry jar with an artful collage of map pieces, photos, and postcards, then embellish with rubber stamps. It's the perfect place to store a variety of long-handled brushes, tubes, and tools.

By Patty Cox

INSTRUCTIONS

Paint:

1. Paint the inside of the pot with Aqua. Let dry.

2. Spray inside of pot with acrylic sealer.

Decoupage & Stamp:

1. Cut or tear vertical sections of the map into 2"-wide strips.

2. Brush a 3"-wide vertical area of decoupage finish on pot. Dip a strip of the old map in water to soften. Press out excess water by passing it between your fingers. Place the map strip on the pot. Brush over map with a generous amount of decoupage finish. Work out wrinkles with fingers. Brush away excess finish.

3. Continue decoupaging strips around pot to cover the entire pot. Don't neglect the areas inside the holes - brush with medium, fold over map strips, and tear away excess. Let dry.

4. Cut out images from old postcards and photographs. Decoupage on areas of map.

5. Cut out small triangles from black paper. Decoupage on the corners of selected photos. Let dry.

6. Rubber stamp a compass and postmarks around caddy with black ink. ❑

SUPPLIES

Pot:

12" standard clay pot

Paints & Finishes:

Outdoor gloss acrylic enamels:

  Barn Red

  Fairway Green

  Ink Blue

  Mustard

  Oxblood

  Twig

Tools & Other Supplies:

Silver metal tape (to plug drainage hole)

Flat artist brushes in assorted widths

Foam brush for base painting

Citronella candles *or* lanterns *or* torches

Sand *or* pea gravel

Pencil and ruler

CARRYING A TORCH
outdoor torch holder

Use flat paint brushes of different widths to create horizontal stripes reminiscent of awning fabric on this colorful pot. Sand or pea gravel safely holds patio torches or candles.

By Patty Cox

INSTRUCTIONS

1. Base paint outside of pot with Mustard. Let dry.

2. Measure and mark increments around the pot with a pencil, spacing the marks about 2" apart.

3. Load flat brush with paint color. Paint stripe around pot sides. Use a different width flat brush with another paint color. Paint stripe around pot sides. Repeat stripes and colors. Let dry.

4. Press a piece of silver tape over the drainage hole on the inside of the pot.

5. Pour sand or gravel in pot.

6. Insert candles or lanterns in sand. ❑

SUPPLIES

Pots:

1 clay pot with ridged sides, 6"

1 clay pot, 2-1/2"

5 clay pots, 2"

Paints & Finishes:

Acrylic craft paints:

    Apricot

    Buttercream

    Green Dark

    Green Light

    Warm White

Acrylic matte sealer spray

Tools & Other Supplies:

Foam brush

Masking tape, 1/2" wide

2 washers, 1-1/2"

Hemp twine

6 large beads

Clear waterproof glue

Drill and 1/4" glass and tile drill bit
    with arrowhead design

Scissors

Ruler

Artist brush, #3 round

SOUNDS IN THE BREEZE
wind chime

By Kathi Bailey

INSTRUCTIONS

Mark & Drill:

1. Make five equally spaced marks around the rim of the large pot for hanging the twine.
2. Drill holes.

Paint:

1. Paint large pot with Buttercream.
2. Using the photo as a guide, apply masking tape to alternate ridges on the large pot to make wide and narrow stripes around pot. Paint wide stripes with Apricot. Paint narrow stripes with Green Light, leaving a Buttercream stripe on either side of the green stripes.
3. Paint small pots and medium pot with Green Light rims and Apricot bodies.
4. Paint leaves and vines on all pots with Green Dark, using round brush. Use photo and patterns as a guide for painting leaves and vine. Let dry.

Finish & Assemble:

1. Spray all pots with matte finish. Let dry.
2. Glue a washer to each side of hole on large pot. Cut 60" of hemp twine. Double and thread through hole. Double knot at top and bottom, leaving 10" to thread through medium pot. Knot twine and attach bead to bottom through medium pot. Knot. Cut off excess.
3. Cut five 15" lengths of hemp. Double and knot through holes around base of large pot. Thread through holes in small pots. Knot. Add beads and knot. Cut off excess hemp twine. ❏

Patterns appear on pages 76 and 77.

Instructions begin on page 75.

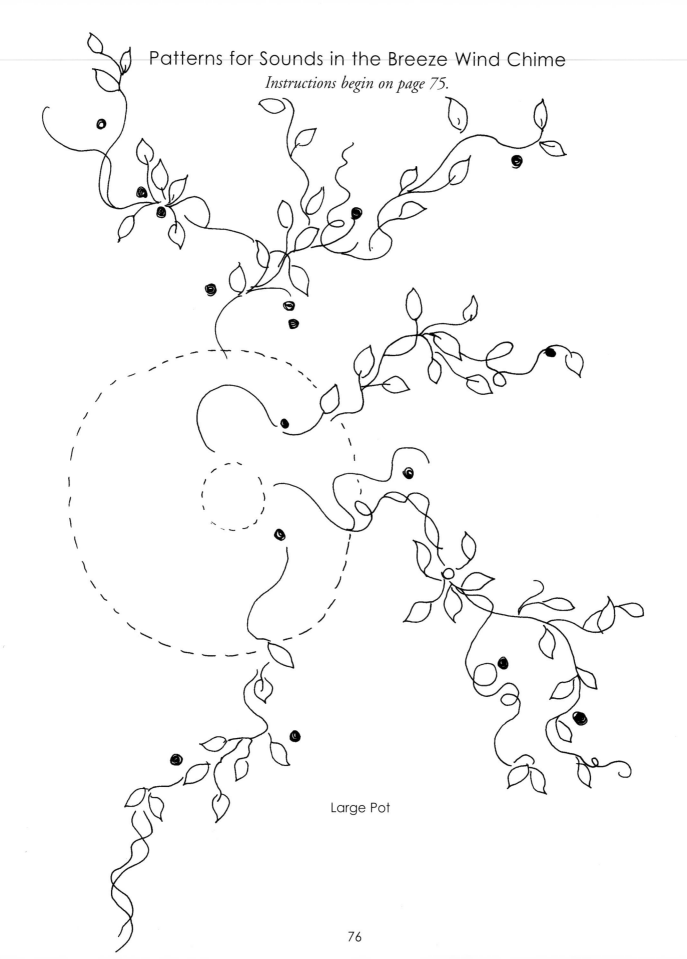

Large Pot

Pattern for Bathroom Helper Washcloth Holder

Instructions begin on page 79.

Forget not that the earth delights to feel your bare feet and the winds long to play with your hair... Kahlil Gibran

Patterns for Sounds in the Breeze Wind Chime

Instructions begin on page 75.

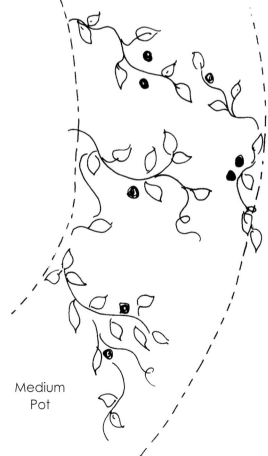

Medium Pot

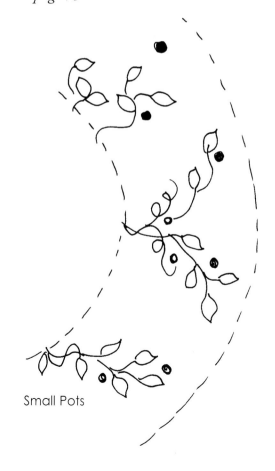

Small Pots

The earth delights to feel your bare feet and the...

SUPPLIES

Pot:

Azalea pot, 8-1/2"

Paints:

Outdoor gloss acrylic enamel
  paints:
  Dolphin Gray
  Patina
  Real Denim

Tools & Other Supplies:

Artist brushes, #1 liner, 1/4" flat,
  1/2" flat, 1/8" flat

Foam brush for base painting

18 shells, 1"

Cobalt blue sea glass

Strong multi-purpose adhesive

Adhesive tile grout

Sponge

Bowl of water

Scouring pad

Transfer paper, tracing paper, and
  stylus

Craft stick

Paper towels

BATHROOM HELPER
washcloth holder

By Patty Cox

INSTRUCTIONS

Paint:

1. Base paint top rim and inside of pot with Real Denim using the foam brush.

2. Base paint remainder of pot with Patina using the foam brush. Let dry.

3. Measure and mark pot in the following order using light pencil lines, from just under rim to bottom: 1/2" area leave Patina, 1/4" Dolphin Gray stripe, 1/2" Patina, 1/4" Denim stripe, 1" Patina area for lettering, 1/4" Denim stripe, 1" Dolphin Gray area, 2" area for sea glass, 1" Denim, remainder Patina. *Note: pots vary in height. Adjust the size of stripes to fit your pot.*

4. Use the 1/4" flat brush to paint the 1/4" wide stripes.

5. Use the 1/2" flat brush to paint the remaining stripes.

6. Transfer lettering to marked area.

7. Paint lettering Dolphin Gray using the liner brush. Let dry.

Decorate:

1. Glue shells onto rim using adhesive.

2. Glue sea glass pieces in marked area all around pot. Allow glue to dry.

3. Press adhesive tile grout between sea glass with a craft stick. Use the craft stick like a trowel to press the top and bottom edges of the grout evenly. Sponge water on sea glass and smooth grout with your fingers, wearing protective gloves. Wipe excess grout off sea glass with a paper towel. Let dry.

4. Scrub grout haze off sea glass with a scouring pad. ❑

Patterns appear on page 77.

SUPPLIES

Pot:

Standard clay pot, 5"

Paints:

Acrylic craft paints:

Aqua

Wicker White

Yellow Citron

Tools & Other Supplies:

Artist brush, 3/4" flat

Foam brush for base painting

Clear-drying white glue

2 strands decorative fibers,
3 yds. each

DESK BUDDY
pencil container

The techniques used to decorate this pot can be adapted to any color scheme. You could also substitute fringe or braid for the fibers.

By Barbara Mansfield

INSTRUCTIONS

Paint:

1. Paint entire pot with Wicker White using foam brush.
2. Load brush with Yellow Citron and slip/slap paint on pot below the rim using the flat brush.
3. Load flat brush with Aqua and paint rim and inside. Allow to dry thoroughly.

Decorate Rim:

Apply glue to rim of pot. Turn pot upside down, wrap the strands of fibers around pot, and press into the glue to adhere. Allow to dry. Turn right side up. ❏

DRAGONFLY LIGHTS
votive candle holders

By Barbara Mansfield

SUPPLIES

Pots:

2 standard clay pots, 2-1/2"

Paints:

Acrylic craft paints:

    Engine Red

    Inca Gold (metallic)

    Pure Orange

    Red Light

    Turner's Yellow

    Wicker White

Acrylic matte sealer spray

Tools & Other Supplies:

Artist brushes - #2 filbert, #4 bristle stippler, 2/0 liner

Foam brush for base painting

Leaf motif stencil (optional)

Transfer paper, tracing paper and stylus

INSTRUCTIONS

1. Paint pots with Wicker White using foam brush. Let dry.

2. Dip 1/3 end of stippler brush in Engine Red, 1/3 in Pure Orange, and 1/3 in Red Light. Stipple the entire pot including the inside with this mix, turning brush with each pounce for variety. Let dry.

3. Either cut stencil for leaf motif for rim or transfer leaf pattern to rim for painting.

4. Transfer patterns for dragonflies to bottom of pots.

5. Load filbert brush with Turner's Yellow. Paint dragonflies. Let dry. Load filbert with Inca Gold. Overstroke dragonflies.

6. Line up leaf edge of stencil with tops of pots. Pounce on Turner's Yellow using stippler or paint design.

7. Load liner brush with inky Licorice. Loosely outline dragonflies. Let dry.

8. Spray with sealer. ❑

Patterns for Dragonfly Lights Votive Candle Holders

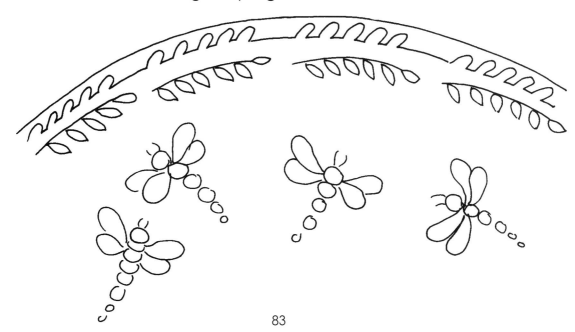

SUPPLIES

Pot:

Terra cotta rose pot, 4"

Paints:

Acrylic craft paints:

    Brilliant Ultramarine

    Fuchsia

    School Bus Yellow

    Wicker White

Acrylic matte sealer spray

Tools & Other Supplies:

Artist brushes - #2 filbert, #4 bristle stippler, 2/0 liner

Foam brush for base painting

BEAUTY HELPER
cosmetic brush holder

The tall shape of a rose pot is just right for storing cosmetic brushes and pencils, keeping them close at hand and easy to find.

By Barbara Mansfield

INSTRUCTIONS

1. Paint pot with Wicker White using foam brush. Let dry.

2. Load stippler with Brilliant Ultramarine and stipple entire pot. Let dry.

3. Load filbert with School Bus Yellow. Paint flower petals and comma strokes on rim.

4. Dip liner brush in Fuchsia and dot flower centers. Let dry.

5. Dip liner brush in Wicker White and dot flower centers, making a smaller dot. Let dry.

6. Spray with acrylic sealer.

Patterns for Beauty Helper
Cosmetic Brush Holder

SUPPLIES

Pot & Saucer:

4" orchid pot

6" clay saucer

Paints, Mediums & Finishes:

Acrylic craft paints:

　Blue Sapphire (metallic)

　Blue Topaz (metallic)

　Plum Pearl (metallic)

　Rose Pearl (metallic)

Acrylic enamel paints:

　Black

　Gold

Glazing medium

Gloss sealer

Tools & Other Supplies:

Foam brush for base painting

Artist brush, 1/2" flat

Black India ink

Gold ink

4 wooden ball knobs, 1"

Strong multi-purpose adhesive

Sewing thread

Old toothbrush (for spattering)

Tall can

RAKU SUNSET
lantern or potpourri holder

An orchid pot, which has three holes on the sides, is used for this lantern. The extra holes also make it a suitable container for potpourri.

By Patty Cox

INSTRUCTIONS

Paint Pot:

1. Paint inside of pot with Gold enamel using foam brush.

2. Paint pot rim with Blue Sapphire.

3. Paint an area below rim with Rose Pearl.

4. Paint below Rose Pearl area with Blue Topaz.

5. Using the 1/2" flat brush, blend the two colors together where they meet.

Glaze & Ink:

1. On a covered work surface, place pot upside down on a tall can. Generously coat outside of pot with glazing medium. While glaze is wet, spatter gold ink around pot, using an old toothbrush, allowing ink to drip in the wet glaze. Let dry.

2. Apply another generous coat of glazing medium to pot. While glaze is wet, slide a piece of thread through a small puddle of black ink. Touch thread to pot and remove - the ink will leave a thin line on the pot that will drip in the wet glaze. Continue applying black thread lines around pot. Let dry.

Finish:

1. Paint entire saucer with Black enamel.

2. Paint wooden balls with Plum Pearl. Let dry.

3. Glue wooden balls on saucer base.

4. Spray pot and saucer with gloss sealer. Let dry. ❏

SUPPLIES

Pot & Saucer:

Round clay pot, 9"

Clay saucer, 7-1/2"

Paints:

Acrylic craft paints:

Antique Copper (metallic)

Black

Copper (metallic)

Gold (metallic)

Teal Pearl

Tools & Other Supplies:

Foam brush for base painting

Ultra thick embossing powder (sold where rubber stamp supplies are available)

Heat gun (to use with embossing powder)

Sea sponge

Spray bottle filled with rubbing alcohol

Handle hardware (a lamp finial, drawer pull, or curtain tieback)

Pizza pan

Aluminum foil

48 oz. juice can

Work surface for using embossing powder

TORTOISESHELL ART
covered container

This covered dish was coated with ultra thick embossing powder. An alternative finish, such as several coats of gloss polyurethane, could also be used.

By Patty Cox

INSTRUCTIONS

1. Paint pot with Teal Pearl using foam brush. Let dry.

2. Prepare a work surface by covering the pizza pan with aluminum foil. Place the juice can at the center of the pan to hold the inverted pot. Place pot upside down over juice can. See photo.

3. Lightly sponge Black, Copper, Antique Copper, and Gold around domed half of pot.

4. While sponged areas are wet, spray rubbing alcohol around the pot. Allow wet paint to drip over sides.

5. Sprinkle embossing powder on damp paint. Melt embossing powder with a heat gun. (The first coat will be bumpy.)

6. Add another coat of embossing powder while the first coat is sticky. Melt the second coat with heat gun. (The second coat will be smooth.) Let cool.

7. Paint the clay saucer with Black, leaving the inside unpainted. Let dry.

8. Attach handle hardware through the hole in bottom of pot. Place pot upside down on saucer. ❑

cream butter sauce
1/4 cup cream
1/3 cup unsalted butter
1/4 tsp salt
pinch of white pepper
3 tbsp lemon juice

appetizers

goat cheese tart - basil pesto, goat
cheese, puff pastry

caponata - roasted eggplant and
peppers a caper marinade

clam cape cod - new england
clams steamed in lemon garlic

mozzarella tomato - tomatoes,
mozzarella, raspberry vinaigrette

portabello mushrooms
with greens and tom

roasted garlic dressing
10 garlic cloves
1 cup olive oil
1 egg yolk
1 tsp dijon mustard
1 minced anchovy
wine vinegar
dash salt
dash white pepper

desserts

pecan cake - with whipped
cream and fresh peaches

chocolate mousse - rich
topped with chocolate shav
and raspberry sauce

flan almonde - light crea

SUPPLIES

Pot:

1 gallon clay strawberry pot

Paints & Finishes:

Acrylic craft paint:

   Black

Decoupage finish, sepia-tone

Acrylic matte sealer

Tools & Other Supplies:

Take-home restaurant menus

Matchbooks from restaurants

Decoupage scissors

Dark brown permanent marker

Blender pen *or* rubbing alcohol and
   cotton swab

Rubber stamp, swirl design

Gold stamp pad

KITCHEN HELPER
utensil caddy

By Patty Cox

INSTRUCTIONS

Paint & Seal:

1. Paint the inside of the pot with Black. Let dry.

2. Spray inside with clear acrylic sealer.

Decoupage:

1. Tear menus into strips.

2. Brush decoupage finish on pot, working one 5" area at a time. Dip a strip of the menu in water to soften. Press out the excess water between your fingers. Place menu strip on pot. Brush over menu with a generous amount of decoupage finish. Work out wrinkles with your fingers. Brush away excess finish.

3. Continue decoupaging strips to cover entire pot. For areas inside holes, brush with decoupage medium, fold over the menu strip, and tear away excess. Let dry.

4. Copy matchbook covers on a color copier. Cut out images. Decoupage images on areas of pot. Let dry. *Option:* To use an actual matchbook on your decoupaged pot, soak the matchbook in water for about five minutes. Separate the top layer from the card stock and decoupage the top layer.

Finish:

1. Outline matchbooks with brown marker. Soften edges with blender pen.

2. Rubber stamp metallic gold swirls around caddy. Let dry. ❏

SUPPLIES

Pot:

Large clay pot

Paints & Finishes:

Acrylic craft paints:

    Black

    Bubble Gum

    Light Pink

    Valentine Pink

    White

Outdoor varnish

Tools & Other Supplies:

Artist brush - 3/4" flat

Foam brush for base painting

Stencil brush

Stencil blank material

Craft knife

Fine tip marker

PRINCESS TREASURES
toy container

By Kirsten Jones

INSTRUCTIONS

1. Paint inside and rim of pot with White using foam brush. Let dry.

2. Paint pot below rim with Black using foam brush. Let dry.

3. Paint alternating vertical stripes with Valentine Pink, Light Pink, and Bubble Gum around the rim, using the 3/4" brush. Let dry.

4. Trace a 1-1/2" circle on stencil blank material. Cut out.

5. Stencil dots randomly on black area of pot with Valentine Pink. Let dry. If needed, stencil a second coat to cover black.

6. Varnish. Let dry. ❑

SUPPLIES

Pot:

3 gallon clay strawberry pot

Paints & Finishes:

Outdoor acrylic enamel paint - Mustard

Acrylic craft paints:

Dark Green

Light Green

Medium Green

Oxblood

Pale Yellow

Terra Cotta

Acrylic sealer

Tools & Other Supplies:

Artist brushes, 3/4" flat, 1/2" flat, #1 liner

Foam brush for base painting

Transfer paper, tracing paper, and stylus

Optional: Foam cushion (to place in bottom of pot)

ENTRY ORGANIZER
umbrella stand

By Patty Cox

INSTRUCTIONS

Paint:

1. Base paint outside of pot with Mustard using foam brush. Let dry.

2. Paint Terra Cotta stripe along pot top and bottom of pot using one of the flat brushes. Let dry.

3. Transfer leaf pattern around pot.

4. Paint the right side of each leaf with Dark Green using 3/4" flat brush. Add large strokes of Medium Green and Light Green on wet paint using 1/2" flat brush. Add a Dark Green outline along the leaf's edge using liner.

5. Paint the left side of each leaf with Light Green. Add large strokes of Medium Green and Pale Yellow on wet paint.

6. Sideload the 3/4" flat brush with Oxblood. Float a shadow around the left edge of each leaf.

7. Float Oxblood along each edge of terra cotta stripes using the 1/2" flat brush. Let dry.

Finish:

1. Spray with acrylic sealer. Let dry.

2. *Option:* Cut a 6" foam circle. Place inside pot. ❏

Pattern appears on page 96.

Pattern for Entry Organizer Umbrella Stand

Enlarge pattern @118% for actual size.

Instructions begin on page 95.

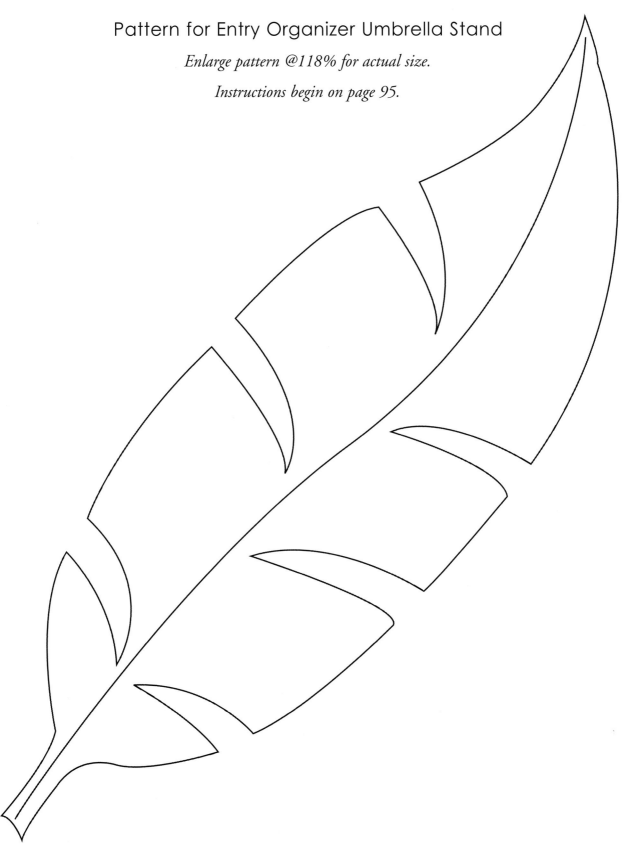

Patterns for Jewels & Sparkles Candle Holders

Instructions begin on page 99.

SUPPLIES

Pots:

2 rose clay pots, 5-1/2" tall

2 wide clay pots, 2-1/2"

2 wide clay pots, 1-1/2"

Paints, Mediums & Finishes:

Acrylic craft paints:

    Fresh Foliage

    Green Forest

    Light Lavender

    Tapioca

    Violet Pansy

Crackle medium

Gold paint pen

Acrylic matte sealer spray

Tools & Other Supplies:

White craft glue

12" purple beaded trim

2 dozen small purple fabric roses

Artist brushes - 1" flat wash, 1/2" angled shader, #5 round

Transfer paper, tracing paper, and stylus

White hologram glitter

JEWELS & SPARKLES
candle holders

By Karen Embry

INSTRUCTIONS

Crackle & Assemble:

1. Brush crackle medium on the pots below the rims. When the crackle medium is tacky to the touch, brush on one coat of Tapioca. Let dry completely.
2. Glue the 2-1/2" pots upside down on top of the upside down rose pots. Glue the 1-1/2" pots, right side up, on top.

Paint:

1. Paint the rim of the top pot and the rim of the bottom pot with Light Lavender. Float the edges with Violet Pansy.
2. Paint the rim of the middle pot with Fresh Foliage. Float the edge with Green Forest. Let dry.
3. Transfer the designs (page 97).
4. Paint the squares in the designs with Light Lavender. Float one edge with Violet Pansy.
5. Paint the hearts in the designs with Fresh Foliage. Float the edges with Green Forest. Let dry.

Finish:

1. Spray with matte acrylic sealer. Let dry.
2. Outline the hearts, squares, and design elements with the gold paint pen.
3. Glue the beaded trim just under the rim of the top pot on each candle holder. ❏

Culinary
Pots

Clay pots are right at home in the kitchen and on the table as containers for food gifts, as serving pieces, or as tabletop accessories. Food can be placed directly on or in unsealed, unpainted clay, but it should not come in contact with paint or chemical sealers. To be safe when serving or storing food on decorated surfaces, use a plastic or glass plate, a plastic liner, or a plastic bag.

Pictured at right: Happy Holidays Gift Container. Instructions begin on page 102.

SUPPLIES

Pots & Saucer:

1 clay pot, 8"

4 clay pots, 1-1/2"

1 clay saucer, 7"

Paints, Mediums & Finishes:

Acrylic craft paints:

    Azure Blue

    Baby Pink

    Black

    Bright Red (metallic)

    Burnt Sienna

    Cappuccino

    Forest Green

    Fresh Foliage

    Gold (metallic)

    Hot Pink

    Light Lavender

    Patina

    Pure Orange

    Tangerine

    Violet Pansy

    Yellow Light

Acrylic matte sealer spray

Tools & Other Supplies:

Artist brushes - #5 round, 1/4"
    angled shader, 10/0 liner

Foam brush for base painting

2 ft. beaded red trim

White craft glue

Transfer paper, tracing paper, and
    stylus

HAPPY HOLIDAYS
gift container

By Karen Embry

INSTRUCTIONS

Paint:

1. Paint all the pots with Gold. Let dry.

2. Transfer the design.

3. Basecoat the Christmas trees with Fresh Foliage. Float one side of each tree with Forest Green.

4. Paint the stars with Yellow Light. Float with English Mustard.

5. Paint some of the ornaments with Baby Pink. Float them with Hot Pink.

6. Paint other ornaments on the tree with Light Lavender. Float them with Violet Pansy.

7. Paint the remaining ornaments on the tree with Tangerine. Float them with Pure Orange.

8. Paint the tree trunks with Cappuccino. Float them with Burnt Sienna.

9. Paint the "swirly" ribbon between the trees with Black.

10. Paint the top half of the rim on the large pot and the saucer with Bright Red metallic. Let dry.

Pattern for Happy Holidays Gift Container

Finish:

1. Glue the four small pots to the bottom of the saucer.

2. Spray all the pots with matte sealer. Let dry.

3. Glue the beaded trim to the edge of the saucer, using the photo as a guide.

To use: Place a cellophane or plastic bag in the pot. Fill with cookies, nuts, or other treats. Secure top of bag with a twist tie, then add a bow. ❏

SUPPLIES

Pot:

Tall clay pot, 8"

Paints, Mediums & Finishes:

Acrylic craft paint:

Linen

Antiquing medium:

Dark Brown

Acrylic matte sealer spray

Tools & Other Supplies:

Anaglyptic wallpaper with leaf motifs (wallpaper with raised pattern but no color)

Scissors

Foam brush

White craft glue (as needed)

Cellulose sponge

Sandpaper

LOVELY LOAVES
bread pot

By Kathy Bailey

INSTRUCTIONS

Adhere Wallpaper:

1. Cut out motifs from wallpaper to fit around base of pot.

2. Adhere motifs to pot, following manufacturer's instructions. Use craft glue as needed to adhere any places that are not firmly attached. Let dry thoroughly.

Paint & Distress:

1. Basecoat entire pot and wallpaper with Linen. Let dry.

2. Sand entire pot, removing most of the paint on the rim. Wipe away dust.

Antique:

Dampen sponge. Apply antiquing medium over pot, applying the medium heavier on the rim. Let dry.

Finish:

Spray with matte sealer. Let dry.

To use: Line with a linen napkin or dish towel. Use for serving bread or breadsticks. ❑

SUPPLIES

Pot & Saucer:

Clay rose pot, 5-1/2"

Clay saucer, 10"

Paints:

Acrylic craft paints:

    Aqua

    Brilliant Ultramarine

    Engine Red

    Inca God (metallic)

    Licorice

    School Bus Yellow

    Yellow Citron

Acrylic matte sealer

Tools & Other Supplies:

Artist brushes - #10 flat,
    1/2" filbert rake, 2/0 liner

Water container

Paper towels

MODERN ART
cake stand

To use this cake stand with food, leave the inside of the saucer unpainted, or place cake on another plate before placing on stand. The painted surface is not food safe.

By Barbara Mansfield

INSTRUCTIONS

1. Using all the colors listed except Inca Gold and Licorice, make random strokes using the #10 flat brush until the surface is covered and pleasing.

2. Load flat brush with Licorice and paint rims of pot and saucer.

3. Load liner with Licorice. Paint lines to form rectangles randomly, using the photo as a guide.

4. Load the filbert rake with Inca Gold and brush over some yellow areas.

5. Highlight rims with Inca Gold. Let dry.

6. Apply sealer to painted area. ❏

ART OF SNACKING
snack server

What a clever way to serve snacks. You can create one for every occasion - black and orange for Halloween, red and green for Christmas, etc. It is inexpensive to make and fun to create. Paint is not foodsafe - be sure to place a clear glass plate on painted surface of saucer. Leave inside of pot unpainted.

By Barbara Mansfield

SUPPLIES

Pot & Saucer:

Clay rose pot, 3"

Clay saucer, 10"

Paints:

Acrylic craft paints:

Aqua

Hot Pink

Patina

Pure Orange

Wicker White

Acrylic sealer

Tools & Other Supplies:

Aartist brushes - #2 and #8 filberts, #4 bristle stippler, 2/0 liner

Round foam-tipped applicator, 5/8"

INSTRUCTIONS

1. Paint pot and saucer with Wicker White. Let dry.
2. Load stippler with Patina and stipple inside of pot, inside of saucer, and rim of saucer. Let dry.
3. Load stippler with Aqua. Paint outside of pot and outside of saucer.
4. Dry brush a few swirls with Aqua inside the saucer. Let dry.
5. Load the #8 filbert with Pure Orange and paint rim of pot and saucer.
6. Load round foam-tipped applicator with Hot Pink. Make random dots on the inside and outside of the saucer and on the outside of the pot.
7. Load the liner with Hot Pink and paint some swirls inside the saucer. Repeat with Pure Orange. Let dry.
8. Apply sealer to painted areas. ❏

RECIPE FOR HAPPINESS
serving stand

The whimsical lettering on the serving stand is a recipe for happiness written in curlicue letters using two different permanent markers. Use the thicker point pen for the "ingredients" (love, laughter, faith, friends, family, etc.) and the thinner point pen for the instructions.

You can do the lettering freehand, using the pattern provided as a guide, or transfer the patterns and trace over the letters. The lettering can also be painted using a liner brush and black acrylic paint or the letters can be rubber stamped using permanent ink.

By Patty Cox

Instructions begin on page 112.

e, Add Laughter. Recipe for 2

cups forgive
art **faith**, 5 go
amily and friend
ter. Mix Well. B
ve **generously.**
ping cups Love, 2 t
ess, Blend **family**

SUPPLIES

Pot & Saucer:

Standard clay pot, 4-1/4"

Clay saucer, 12-1/4"

Paints & Finishes:

Outdoor gloss acrylic enamel -
　Mustard, *optional* Black

Acrylic matte sealer spray

Tools & Other Supplies:

Foam brush for base painting

Strong multi-purpose adhesive

Permanent marking pens,
　.01 and .03

Optional: Transfer paper and stylus,
　liner brush, alphabet rubber
　stamps and permanent ink pad

RECIPE FOR HAPPINESS
serving stand

INSTRUCTIONS

1. Turn pot upside down. Center and glue the clay saucer on top of the overturned pot. Let dry.

2. Paint pot stand and underside of saucer with Mustard, leaving the top lip and inside of saucer unpainted. Let dry.

3. Write the Recipe for a Happy Life around the pot and saucer, using the two markers. Abbreviate words as needed, such as teaspoon to tsp., to fit. *Options:* Transfer lettering and trace over with markers *or* transfer letters and paint with Black paint, using a liner brush *or* rubber stamp with permanent ink. Let dry.

4. Spray the painted and written parts - but not the rim or inside of the saucer - with clear acrylic sealer. Let dry.

To use: Place food on unpainted, unsealed saucer for serving. Don't let food touch the painted areas. ❏

Pattern for Recipe for Happiness Serving Stand

Recipe for a happy life, 1 bushel of family and friends.

1 heaping cup of love.

3 cups forgiveness.

2 tablespoons hope, 1 quart faith, 5 gallons laughter.

Blend family and friends with love, forgiveness, hope and faith.

Add laughter and mix well.

Bake with sunshine. Serve generously.

SUPPLIES

Pots:

Tall clay pot, 7"

Clay saucer, 6"

Paints, Mediums & Finishes:

Acrylic craft paint:

Cappuccino

Stencil gel paints:

Fern Green

Hunter Green

Napa Grape

High gloss brush-on sealer

Acrylic matte sealer spray

Decoupage finish

Tools & Other Supplies:

Foam brush for base painting

Stencil brushes

Sponge brushes

Scissors

Stencil pre-cut with grape motifs

Wine quotations printed on cream paper

3 wooden ball knobs, 1-1/4" (for feet)

Clear waterproof glue (construction adhesive *or* silicone)

KEEP IT COOL
wine cooler

By Kathi Bailey

INSTRUCTIONS

Prepare Pot:

1. Clean pot and saucer with vinegar and water. Let dry thoroughly.

2. Spray inside and outside with matte sealer spray.

Paint:

1. Paint pot, saucer, and wooden ball feet with Cappuccino using foam brush.

2. Use a stencil brush to apply Napa Grape paint to rim of pot, rim of saucer, and clay feet. Let dry.

Glue:

1. Glue knobs to bottom of saucer for feet.

2. Glue pot inside saucer. Let dry overnight.

Stencil:

1. Stencil grapes with Fern Green and Napa Grape.

2. Stencil leaves with Fern Green and Hunter Green.

Decoupage & Finish:

1. Cut out wine quotations. Adhere to pot with decoupage finish. Let dry.

2. Apply two coats of high gloss sealer. Let dry. ❑

PLEASE BE SEATED
table place favors

Use these colorful painted pots with gleaming metallic accents as place cards and party favors. Fill them with sprouted wheatgrass, small potted plants, or bags of candies, mints, or cookies. Hand-letter names on place cards and tape to sticks or skewers. Wheatgrass seed is available at health food stores; to sprout, see below.

By Karen Embry

To grow wheatgrass:

1. Fill 3-1/2" plastic pots with potting soil. Sprinkle soil with wheatgrass seeds and water to dampen the soil.
2. Place the pots in a sunny window and water to keep the soil moist but not soggy. The seeds will sprout in five or six days, sending out straight green shoots.

To use:

1. Place a plastic pot with sprouted grass inside each decorated terra cotta pot.
2. Add place cards. ❑

Instructions for decorating the pots begin on page 118.

SUPPLIES

Pots:

3 wide-top clay pots, 3-1/2"

Paints & Finishes:

Acrylic craft paints:

    Amethyst (metallic)

    Antique Gold (metallic)

    Baby Pink

    Champagne (metallic)

    Dioxazine Purple

    Light Lavender

    Permanent Rose

    Rose Pearl (metallic)

    Wicker White

Floating medium

Acrylic matte sealer spray

Tools & Other Supplies:

3 pieces beaded trim, 12" each
one purple, one pink, one white

Artist brushes - 1" flat wash, 10/0
liner, 1/2" angled shader

Transfer paper, tracing paper, and
stylus

White craft glue

PLEASE BE SEATED
table place favors

Pictured on pages 116-117.

INSTRUCTIONS

Prepare:

1. Paint one pot with Baby Pink, one with Light Lavender, and one with Wicker White. Let dry.

2. Transfer the designs.

Paint the Pink Pot:

1. Float the top edge (under the rim) and the bottom edge of the Baby Pink pot with Rose Pearl. See page 29 for "How to Float."

2. Paint swirls with Rose Pearl.

3. Paint the inside of the swirl with Permanent Rose.

4. Paint the tiny dots around the bottom with Permanent Rose.

Paint the Lavender Pot:

1. Float the top edge (under the rim) and the bottom of the Light Lavender pot with Amethyst.

2. Paint the stars with Amethyst.

Patterns for Please Be Seated Table Place Favors

3. Paint the inside of the stars and the dots at the bottom with Dioxazine Purple.

Paint the White Pot:

1. Float the top edge (under the rim) and the bottom edge of the Wicker White pot with Champagne.

2. Paint the hearts with Champagne.

3. Paint the insides of the hearts with Antique Gold.

Finish:

1. Spray all three pots with matte sealer. Let dry.

2. Glue coordinating trim on each pot. ❏

RETRO KITCHEN
canister set

These red-and-white canisters with retro appeal would be right at home in a mid-20th century kitchen. The dots are stamped with craft foam circles glued to the eraser ends of pencils, a pencil eraser, and the handle end of a brush. The "rick-rack" trim on the rim is painted with a brush.

Though the insides of the pots and saucers are not painted, it's still a good idea to use rigid plastic liners or plastic bags for flour, sugar, and coffee.

By Patty Cox

Instructions begin on page 122

SUPPLIES

Pots & Saucers:

3 standard clay pots, 8"

3 clay saucers, 9"

Paints:

Gloss enamel spray paint - White

Gloss enamel paint - Apple Red

Tools & Other Supplies:

High speed mini drill

3/16" silicone carbide grinding stone bit

3 wooden knobs with screws, 1-1/2"

3 fender washers, 3/16"

Cork from coaster or wine bottle

Art foam

3 new pencils

Artist brushes, 3/4" flat, 1/2" flat, 1/4" flat

Transfer paper and stylus

Stamping tools

RETRO KITCHEN
canister set

Pictured on page 120.

INSTRUCTIONS

Drill:

Drill a 3/16" hole in center of each saucer lid using a silicone carbide grinding stone bit. Wipe away dust.

Paint:

1. Spray outsides of saucer lids and outsides of pots with White. Let dry.

2. Paint bottom 2" of each pot with Apple Red enamel using the 3/4" flat brush.

3. Transfer and paint a wavy line around the top rim of each pot using the 1/2" flat brush.

4. Transfer and paint lettering on each pot using the 1/4" flat brush.

5. Cut a 3/8" circle and a 1/2" circle from craft foam. Glue to ends of two pencils.

6. To make dots, use the handle ends of a paint brush, a pencil eraser, the 3/8" foam circle, and the 1/2" foam circle. (See photo of stamping tools.) Dip in paint. Dot lid and a border around the top of the pot under the rim. Let dry.

7. Paint wooden knobs with Apple Red. Let dry.

Assemble:

1. Insert screws on wooden knobs through holes on lids. Secure using fender washers on the insides of lids.

2. Trace drainage holes of pots on corks. Trim corks. Plug holes in pots. ❑

Patterns for Retro Kitchen Canister Set

DIRT CAKE

This easy-to-make dessert is so clever - cookies, pudding, and whipped cream are layered to create a delicious novelty cake. Serve it for a birthday, a spring gathering, a summer picnic, or a party in your garden - it's sure to delight your guests.

The cake is not baked, so you can use any decorated pot if the inside has not been painted or sealed - and the pot can be washed. Or, if you like, use a plastic container or bowl that fits inside a pot and fill the bottom of the pot with floral foam so the top of the liner is even with the top of the pot. The pot or liner should hold approximately 5 cups.

RECIPE

1. Crush **1 large package chocolate sandwich cookies**. Using a food processor makes the job easier. Set aside.

2. To make filling, combine **2 packages vanilla pudding** with **3 cups milk**. You can use either instant pudding or cooked pudding. Allow cooked pudding to cool.

3. To make topping, combine **8 oz. cream cheese**, **1 cup powdered sugar**, and **2 cups whipped cream or non-dairy frozen whipped cream substitute**.

4. Set aside about 1/2 cup cookie crumbs. Sprinkle half of the remaining crumbs into bottom of container or pot. Place filling on top. Sprinkle remaining half of crumbs on top of filling.

5. Smooth topping over filling.

6. Sprinkle the reserved 1/2 cup of cookie crumbs on the topping. ❏

The "dirt" cake was placed in a bowl that fit into decorated pot.

See page 66 for instructions to create the Happy Birthday pot.

125

FLOWER POT BREAD

Unglazed terra cotta is especially nice for baking bread because it holds moisture. The unique shape of a clay pot makes this bread especially nice for gift giving or parties. To make this Flower Pot Bread, use any yeast bread recipe. You can even cheat and use frozen bread dough - your friends and family won't know the difference, and they will think you are so clever.

If you plan to give the bread as a gift, remove the bread from the pot it was baked in, allow to cool, and then place in a fresh, clean pot.

PROCEDURE

1. Thoroughly wash and dry the pot.

2. Soak the pot in warm water overnight or until it has soaked up a good amount of moisture. Dry the inside.

3. Preheat oven according to your bread recipe.

4. Cut several rounds of **aluminum foil** to fit the bottom of the pot and cover the hole.

5. Coat the inside of the pot with **butter or shortening**.

6. Place **bread dough** in pot - it should fill two-thirds of the pot. Allow to rise until doubled.

7. Bake according to your recipe or until top is golden. ❑

Tips for Baking in Terra Cotta

People have been using terra cotta vessels for cooking since ancient times. You can buy unglazed terra cotta pots, baking pans, and roasters from kitchen stores and online retailers or improvise with clay pots and saucers. They are wonderful for baking and for roasting meats - no special recipes are required. You soak the pot in water before baking, and during the baking process the water evaporates from the pores of the clay, keeping the juices contained.

Here are some tips for getting started with terra cotta cooking:

- Don't use terra cotta on top of the stove.

- When roasting, use a hotter temperature (100 degrees hotter than the recipe calls for) and allow more time.

- Soak the pot and lid in water, drain, place the food inside, cover, and place in oven.

- To clean the pot after use, let cool and soak in warm water. To remove dried-on food, sprinkle with salt and scrub with a stiff brush. Rinse and let dry. Do not use detergents, soaps, or scouring powder, and don't wash in the dishwasher. To remove any lingering odors from spices or fish, soak in hot water and baking soda. Use 3/4 cup baking soda for each gallon of water.

METRIC CONVERSION CHART

Inches to Millimeters and Centimeters

Inches	MM	CM	Inches	MM	CM
1/8	3	.3	2	51	5.1
1/4	6	.6	3	76	7.6
3/8	10	1.0	4	102	10.2
1/2	13	1.3	5	127	12.7
5/8	16	1.6	6	152	15.2
3/4	19	1.9	7	178	17.8
7/8	22	2.2	8	203	20.3
1	25	2.5	9	229	22.9
1-1/4	32	3.2	10	254	25.4
1-1/2	38	3.8	11	279	27.9
1-3/4	44	4.4	12	305	30.5

Yards to Meters

Yards	Meters
1/8	.11
1/4	.23
3/8	.34
1/2	.46
5/8	.57
3/4	.69
7/8	.80
1	.91
2	1.83
3	2.74
4	3.66
5	4.57
6	5.49
7	6.40
8	7.32
9	8.23
10	9.14

INDEX